TREES ARE BRIDGES TO THE SKY

Trees are Bridges to the Sky

Frederick Livingston

WAYFARER
BASED IN THE BERKSHIRE MOUNTAINS, MASS.

WAYFARER

BASED IN THE BERKSHIRE MOUNTAINS, MASS.

Published in 2024 by Homebound Publications & Wayfarer Books
Cover Design and Interior Design by Connor Wolfe
TRADE PAPERBACK 978-1-956368-84-0
Also Available in eBook

10 9 8 7 6 5 4 3 2 1

Look for our titles wherever books are sold.
Wholesale offerings for retailers available through Ingram.

PO Box 1601, Northampton, MA 01060

860.574.5847 | info@homeboundpublications.com

HOMEBOUNDPUBLICATIONS.COM & WAYFARERBOOKS.ORG

Are humans parasites, sowing our own hunger
or fruit, gifts from Earth to our future?
Is the edge of our lives, civilization, and species
a cliff to catastrophe, or a bridge to transformation?

The future begins with seeds we plant in this moment.

DEDICATION

To the humans who first showed me the forest:
my mother, uncle Jim, and all the other teachers.

CONTENTS

Seeds

Parasites

Fruit

Humus

Eco crisis:

our only home,

unraveling

"Until you dig a hole, you plant a tree, you water it and make it survive, you haven't done a thing. You are just talking."

—WANGARI MAATHAI, founder of the Green Belt Movement and 2004 Nobel Peace Prize Laureate

SEEDS

Where future begins

ABSTRACT

I wrote these words not by calculating probability
but because I cannot survive without evolution
or maybe a better word is "blooming."

Or maybe a better world is blooming
from our seeds
I mean
bundled slumber
hope condensed into a precise jewel.

Because if our dreams are not fertile,
why do we wake?

INTRODUCTION

This book grew from the seed of my thesis at the University for Peace. My physical project involved growing and planting hundreds of tropical fruit trees. Accompanying this effort was a report, adapted here.

Initially conceived to offset a lifetime of carbon emissions, my goal gained nuance as I studied my seedlings. I watched trees offer answers to some of the most pressing questions I hear from my students, peers, questions I struggle with myself:

How can we reconcile the smallness of individual action with the scale of global ecocrisis? Are we fated to destroy our only home? Or is the field of human potentiality larger? How are we to live?

I do not believe in definitive answers to these questions, but there is much to learn from how other beings have grappled with similar questions over millions of years.

I conclude the fate of our species hangs on the metaphors we use to place ourselves in the world.

DREAMS

By metaphors, dreams, seeds, I mean no magical thinking, no ghostly fruit of faith without skin or syrup. I am referring to the power of imagination to shape landscapes in its own image.

I mean fences, cut through contiguous systems like the human heart. The gossamer web of laws upon which necks hang or the fallen are caught. Identities we sharpen into blades that spill blood. Bodies we throw into economies to stoke their hungry fires.

Nothing in this world is fixed. Societies have walked away from their masters and forged new cultures to prevent a totalitarian return. The spell breaks when we recognize we arrived here through footsteps, no matter how numerous. We can still walk away, however uncertain the path.

There are lands legally considered forests that contain no trees, trees seen as money are cut, pulped and printed into currency.

If all that is at stake overwhelms you, remember all that remains in the air: we believe the world into being.

SEEDLING

The first metaphor to emerge from my nursery was planting. Over the course of my project, it became clear many variables were beyond my control: insect appetites and changing rains. Others I could control: the attention I gave my seedlings or the humility to learn from mistakes.

After putting trees in the ground and leaving the University for Peace, the project leaves my hands. So I must do everything I can in the moments I do have to ensure at least the possibility of success. This is exactly what a tree does when it makes its own seeds. This is also what I am doing writing this book.

Believing our small actions cannot make a difference may inhibit us from taking the initial step of planting. We forget the undeniable truth that we only exist because of seeds planted up to this moment: from the literal fruits that nourish us to the uncountable efforts of all who came before us.

After the intense effort sowing seeds from our best intentions, follows a long road of growth in an uncertain world.

SUCCESSION

Can one person make a difference?

I do not know the answer, so I ask the humble dandelion. After devastation, a weed does not set out to heal a forest. How would a seed germinate under such pressure?

The dandelion only knows how to anchor its root and hold soil, to spread its rosette over bare ground, sheltering from sun and wind, to drink in whatever moisture it finds, breathing it back into the cloudless sky, and die back in its time, reinvesting the carbon it collected into the soil.

Eventually the harsh earth becomes tolerable
to larger shrubs or perhaps a tiny vole.
Each brings its unique gifts
though they may not live to see their seeds grow.

Soon a moonscape becomes an earthscape:
towering conifers wash the forest in shade.
The air is mild, wet, and fragrant with life:
mosses, ferns, insects, fallen logs, a wealth of possibilities.

Now, do you think the tallest sequoia looks down
on the forest canopy and proclaims
"look at what I have made!"

SERVICES

Even sound science stands on metaphor. The term "ecosystem services" was coined in the 1970s to speak nature in the language of money. We gain numbers, but lose everything outside our business model.

The danger of a language for productive output is that it cannot describe the value of existence. Trees, of course, are more than just the capital they represent when sold for carbon credit or board feet.

You could tally the carbon trees capture,
the soil they build and hold in place,
the rain they bring by their breathing,
the shade, habitat, and nutrients they offer,
their ability to reverse desertification,
reduce violence, stress and mental fatigue,
but never reach the sum of a tree's being.

There is no dollar amount for trees' investment in the project of living, the dividends of wisdom they pay those who listen, the opportunity cost of cutting short the conversation among their roots, of consciousness reaching for sky.

SACRED

Humans have recognized the value of trees for as long as we have memory. Many cultures have identified a "tree of life" in their ecosystem that sustains them with food, medicine, fuel, material for shelter, clothes, transport and more: from the Cedars of the Pacific Northwest to the Baobab of East Africa to the Date Palms of the Middle East and beyond. Their spiritual nourishment is no less consequential.

Hindu scriptures warn of deforestation as a doomsday omen and advise planting trees to avoid hell. Trees are often depicted as bridges between material and spiritual worlds, from the bodhi tree the Buddha sat under to attain enlightenment to the olive branch that signaled dry land to Noah.

Our spiritual connection to trees should not be dismissed as mere superstition. Forests designated as "sacred" are often better protected than forests managed under formal legal mechanisms.

Trees point us towards our higher selves, inviting us to imagine how we too might become, "humans of life".

WAR

A century ago, European farmers preferred the metaphor of a "doctor," tasked with maintaining the health of a crop. Through this lens, diseases and pests could be mitigated by promoting ecological wellbeing.

After World War II, a new metaphor was introduced to utilize the enormous and now unnecessary chemical weapon factories. By shifting the pursuit of health to a "war," it became rational to escalate conflicts between farmers and "enemies" such as insects and nutrient deficiencies. Now strawberries are fumigated with tear gas, weeds are treated with Agent Orange ingredients, nitrogen bombs materials are repurposed as fertilizer, plants grow in soldierly rows... but instead of defeating scarcity, our allies are surrendering: from soil microbes to pollinators, aquifers, even rhythms of rain.

Examples are found across the world, from the "war on drugs" that inspired the Columbian government to spray carcinogenic herbicides across swaths of rainforest, to the "war on poaching" escalating deadly conflict throughout the African continent. All remind us war is not our last resort. War is failure to imagine mutual victory.

Metaphors have the power to shape our culture.
But culture also has the power to shape its metaphors.

SEEDBANK

The human species is endangered many times over. Just one of our many interrelated alarms would be enough to end us, from climate crisis to desertification, extreme social inequality and centuries spent looting a wealth of biological and cultural diversity.

We will not solve our problems next year, because they did not begin last year. Although a tree's trunk and branches may be most obvious to us, just as much biomass may exists below the Earth's surface. Sometimes roots reach deeper than the crown is tall.

Although the problems facing now us are real and urgent, we must recognize that the process of healing will unfold, if it is to unfold at all, over the course of hundreds or thousands of years. This healing is not inevitable. It will depend on which seeds we sow in the field of human potentiality. In this moment, and every moment following.

Everything from poverty to oil spills to war can be seen not as spontaneous outbreaks of misfortune, but as thorns growing in the spaces we failed to sow with love.

CHANGE

Would you consider a seed
lying motionless in soil,
year after year, hopeless?

Weeds now germinating in your garden
 may have been sown before you were born.

Date palm seeds discovered in an archaeological site in Judea
—nearly 2,000 years old—recently sprouted.

One hemlock grew from one seed, now making trillions—
a whole forest and more.

There are species of moss living deep in caves
that grow only one moment each day
when the sun's angle reaches their green tendrils.

There are toads frozen in snow waiting for spring to thaw them back
to life. Cacti are waiting on rains to flower.

An invisible riot of creatures are waiting for longer daylength, enough
heat, dry land, fungal touch, fire, drowning, to be swallowed, a gap in
the canopy—for growth to become possible again.

Yes we ache,
but the human world is no rare exception
where change is always linear, predictable,
or recognizable as it occurs.

SHADE

If there is anything fortunate about unsustainable behavior, it is that it will not survive time. It is unnecessary to debate the permanence of industrial agriculture as we know it, capitalism, or Western hegemony. Our concern is not whether our systems will change, but how they will evolve towards more harm or healing.

We cannot wait to imagine the next world until this one is ashes. When a tree falls in the forest, it is the seedlings already waiting in the shade who answer the sudden light.

If we prepare only for war, from where will peace arise? If we hoard resources in our doomsday shelters, from where will abundance grow?

No matter how thick the canopy, never let it smother your dreams. Germinate them wherever possible so that when an opening comes, as it inevitably will, you are ready.

TREES

While resplendent with benefits, trees will not solve all our problems.

Trees have attracted attention for their utility in carbon offsetting schemes. While the process of trees sequestering carbon is a biological fact, the ability for humans to purchase carbon out of the air through market mechanisms remains unrealized. Trees do not simply "remove" carbon from the atmosphere but hold it in their bodies while they live. Trees may give up to half of the carbon they collect to the soil under ideal conditions, but the rest generally returns to the air when a tree decays or burns.

While trees have the potential to reverse desertification, planting them in some ecosystems, such as a native prairie, can reduce biodiversity and other measures of health. Trees can lower the water table enough to make springs run dry. In regions such as the boreal forests of the arctic circle, the dark color of tree cover absorbs more heat than the reflective white snow, further accelerating warming.

No other species will save humans from the crisis we have caused. This is our work. Trees can be our allies if we open our hearts to listen, or mere tools if we open our hands to take.

FIGURE 1. METAPHORS MAY SAVE US

I mean this literally, existentially:
humans cannot endure as parasites,
thieves, invasive species.

Our only hope is to send
better metaphors under the surface
of our obvious catastrophe

to discover more subtle
subterranean truths with room
for life to continue its bloom.

Shallow truths often contradict
deeper reality. What you
should know about me is

I am mostly empty space
and so are you
and so almost everything

we hold within us
is indistinguishable
and inextinguishable:

ephemeral elements
dreaming solid bodies.
Gently remember, we see nothing

directly. Even God
is a metaphor
for something larger than language.

Metaphors are maps,
not the terrain. Oars in a sea
we will never fully explore.

Metaphors do not arise
from human minds,
like money or hot air balloons.

We encounter them because everything
is interrelated more deeply
than it is distinct.

Metaphors are only darkness between stars,
they will not pull us
from the tombs our tongues have dug.

We must lean into our dreams
bring them to flesh and stone,
become fruit, humus, humans

of life. Even now
in the dark night of soil
seeds are waking.

"What we are doing to the forests of the world is
but a mirror reflection of what we are doing
to ourselves and to one another."

—CHRIS MASER, *Forest Primeval:*
The Natural History of an Ancient Forest

Parasites

Identity precipitates action

NEED

The Earth is an open hand.
Our wrong is not in needful taking,
but in closing our hands around these gifts,
in claiming they belonged to us, damming generous rivers.

Hold this close when considering sacrifices our future requires:

It is not wrong that we eat,
we were given mouths.
It is not wrong to seek shelter
we were given thin skin.
It is not wrong that we travel,
we were given feet and dreams.

It is the means we have chosen towards these ends that share
enormous harm with the living world. Wearing different metaphors,
employing different means, will require creativity, persistence, even
love: nothing less than an evolution of consciousness.

THIEVES

The difference with trees, when in balance, is they claim land not just for themselves, but for all life that follows them. They take what they need and share it with the wider community. They show there is nothing inevitable about a linear supply chain that extracts resources and produces waste.

Industrial culture measures wealth by accumulation: larger houses with larger lawns, increasing appetites for animal products and plastics, how many dollars we take to our grave. Other cultures and creatures have measured wealth by what we have the good fortune to give away.

No living thing grows without an equal amount of decay. When we take more than our share, we simply pass on the necessary sacrifices to other beings. Peace and justice may be perceived as loss by those who profit from violence and domination, but these sacrifices will earn us something no amount of theft can buy: a future.

TRAGEDY

An English countryside is grazed with restraint until the day a clever herder realizes he can add one more sheep at direct benefit to himself. When the neighbors catch on, everyone attempts to enrich themselves by following his example... until the resource is exhausted, and everyone goes hungry.

This "tragedy of the commons" scenario was originally posed by Garett Hardin to explain why welfare recipients' "freedom to breed is intolerable". Although his essay is frequently cited as evidence of humanity's short-sighted greed, the actual herders of England were able to anticipate this phenomenon and put in place cultural practices to promote balance. As all cultures must if they are to endure.

The assumption of failure continues to haunt present-day inhabitants of Easter Island, the Maya, and indigenous societies across the world who have been used as textbook examples of environmental overreach and yet miraculously continue to exist. Despite centuries of devastation at the hands of the very colonizers accusing them of greed.

Declaring a forest "collapsed" makes it much easier to justify its removal, appropriating resources that no longer exist on paper.

BREED

Population has been blamed for societal ills throughout history: from Thomas Malthus' unrealized prediction of global starvation in 1798 to eugenics, racial cleansing and beyond. While not always so specific, many environmentalists continue to lean on this narrative, suggesting the ultimate answer is to reduce our numbers.

Conflating humanity with the harm we have caused, we forget that ecocrisis is not only an equation of bodies, but of how those bodies relate to their environments. If you consider that one American emits as much carbon as 74 Afghanis, or that China emits many times more than the entire continent of Africa, differences in birthrate become less central.

Shifting our focus to consumption, we can stop debating how many children each woman "should" have and investigate the largely male-dominated institutions responsible for the vast majority of ecological damages.

We can stop demanding answers from poor communities with high birth rates and little power, and start asking wealthy nations with a much greater capacity to impact the global carbon balance for the lifestyle changes our planet requires.

FEED

Enough sunlight falls on the surface of Earth to feed each leaf and mouth. Recognizing scarcity as a failure of justice and imagination, we can stop asking the sun for more, and instead explore how we can open ourselves further to receive.

The biointensive method of agriculture, to use one example, can produce a complete diet in about 4,000 square feet per person while improving soil health, saving water, and abandoning our reliance on synthetic pesticides, fertilizer, and heavy machinery. The Earth's arable land could support about 37 billion humans with this rate. Allowing 70% of this productive land to rewild, would still leave us with enough land to feed well beyond the 10 billion people the UN estimates as the peak human population around the year 2080.

Even with current yields, we can already feed peak population if we divert food lost to waste, biofuel, and meat production towards human consumption.

Many viable solutions already exist, but all of them will require radical value shifts. Stay skeptical of any solution that asks you to remain seated, to become comfortable with hunger, from Green Capitalism to Climate Smart genetically modified crops, any repackaged inertia.

CONSERVATION

Labeling humans positive or negative forces is not purely a philosophical exercise, it shapes policies that uproot people. Efforts from wealthy nations to "conserve" healthy ecosystems have often resulted in the forced removal of indigenous communities from landscapes they have actively managed for generations. In inventing pristine nature, we become its opposite.

Clearly not all human action is in service to life, but there is ample evidence much of it is. Indigenous forest-dependent communities have managed to preserve over half of the Earth's biodiversity, despite owning only 11% of its land. It has also been demonstrated that actively managed land can be more productive and contain more biodiversity than adjacent wild spaces. Some wild plants become more prolific after responsible harvesting.

Reuniting with the nature we pretend ourselves separate from requires unearthing roots of self-destructive culture, but it allows us to see ourselves as collaborators in the evolution of consciousness, as much a part of biodiversity as any rare bird or tree frog.

FIGURE 2. EUTROPHICATION

or

An open letter from the Desert Globemallow
after discovering smog from Los Angeles
deposits nitrogen on surrounding landscapes
at levels comparable to agricultural applications

Thank you for your generous gift.
Unfortunately we cannot accept it because our roots
have adapted to desert austerity since before
the city of Los Angeles was imaginable.

Unlike you, we learned to live with
what we were given. By taking more
than you were given you've showed globemallows
something we had never seen before: waste.

We cannot accept your gift
because it was not yours to give.
The nutrients now contaminating our soil
came from your clouds of smog,

which came from your vehicles burning
fuel you exhumed from our ancestors' graves
in order to move more quickly
from point A to point B.

Contemplate this while stuck in your famous traffic,
inside a vehicle designed for speed and freedom:
the dose makes the poison
and you are shoving sugar down our throats.

We don't travel in the desert
because we know there is no heaven
except the one we create ourselves.
We have spun life from sand

with crusts of lichen, cyanobacteria,
archaea and all the other creatures
you register only as the "crunch"
under your foot.

It hasn't rained much in forty years.
You will never accumulate enough wealth
to purchase what we earned
over delicate generations:

the wisdom to live humbly
in this place we both call home.
We will not survive if this continues…
but neither will you.

Good

Consider all the creatures that have become leaders in their ecosystems, keystones of flourishing communities, from sea stars to trees to mycorrhizae. We simply cannot say positive relationships are impossible.

Communities in the Amazon rainforest learned long ago how to build soil with fire, leaving rich earth as a sign of human settlement. Much of the indigenous-managed land European colonizers encountered was so lush they consistently mistook it for untouched wilds.

Many species and cultures have been destroyed, but enough seeds have been saved from the wisdom traditions of the world for the ecological healing ahead of us. The skills to widen spirals of abundance have been carried forward all over the world with new names like agroecology, Indigenous Knowledge, regenerative, biointensive, and permaculture.

We know that humans can cooperate with plants to build healthy soil much faster than would naturally occur, can remove toxins from landscapes, can recharge aquifers, all while feeding ourselves and others.

Accepting this, the harm we have done to our planet can no longer be seen as an inevitable consequence of our nature, but symptoms of an unhealthy worldview.

EVIL

From all that we have broken, willfully, in full view of the suffering in our hands, we cannot say humans are merely ignorant or purely good. It does not serve us to deny the very real evil we have so often brought to each other and to the rest of the living world. There will be no point in the future where our massacres will have been worthwhile, a necessary step towards utopia. No child has ever starved to teach us a lesson about suffering.

What we are left with is not a map towards a promised land, but a scattered pile of bones: the species and cultures that have survived, haunted by memories of our terrible capacities. How we assemble them is indeed an act of imagination. The splash of color or the presence of feathers is beyond solid ground, into a beckoning fog.

No other species will decide for us if humans are good or evil.

We decide our legacy with every seed we sow.

Symbiosis

The divide between mutually beneficial and parasitic relationships is often burdened by judgments of "good and evil", but reality is always more complex than our stories.

Organisms relate across a fluid spectrum of give and take. Many orchids, for example, take nutrients from their hosts while young, but eventually become more generous as they age. Some relationships are still debated: did we domesticate crops to spread civilization, or did crops domesticate us to spread themselves?

Through evolutionary conversation, some parasitic organisms have become mutualists, challenging notions of destiny and serving as evidence that it is also possible for humans to change their relationship to the planet.

Because life is never still.

INNOVATION

A forest cannot regrow until the wildfire is extinguished. There is no way to escape the cultural change necessary for planetary survival.

We will not be able to plant enough trees or wind turbines to stop climate crisis

unless we also cut emissions drastically. We often assume new technologies displace dirtier ones, but this remains largely unrealized.

Innovation is no alternative to the work of inner evolution
because it is our hands that hold our tools
our minds that guide our hands
and our hearts that feed our dreams.

When we invent a carbon capture machine made from locally abundant materials that runs on sunlight, emits water and oxygen, self-replicates and biodegrades, we will still be millions of years behind plants.

Scorched earth has returned to forest
again and again,
but every time it required nothing less
than total reinvention.

EFFICIENCY

When loggers invented the chainsaw,
one could suddenly cut in an afternoon
what two used to do in a week.

Yet this did not result in more leisure time
for lumberjacks. It merely increased the speed
at which we cleared the forests.

Similarly, increasing the efficiency
of an economy designed to strip the Earth bare
may only increase the rate we dismantle the planet.

Now consider all the places we linger.
Imagine efficiency while eating a ripe mango,
in exploring a forest, or making love.

Efficiency strips the rich world into a finitude
of variables that can be maximized, ignoring
the infinite complexity and beauty of life's mystery.

Ask yourself what you want the future to be
full of and let your hands carry it forward.
Let efficiency be just another tool along the way.

VALUES

The market is a language of value. It has no body
other than the tongues and limbs and claws we give it.
To speak of a habitable future, we must value life over consumption.

Measuring a farm's efficiency by how few farmers can pull how
many pounds from the soil with unlimited petrochemical inputs
will exhaust all topsoil in a few decades. Measuring success instead
in pounds of soil created, hunger and waste erased, communities
deepening roots, our nourishment can heal.

It was never inevitable our infrastructure would promote
desertification, pollution, and monotony, instead of celebrating
environmental services and diversity. When we stop accepting toxic
externalities, we can begin our designs from a place efficiency would
never have reached.

We built a culture around personalized internal combustion that
pretends we can get anywhere in this world alone. We could prefer
the pleasure and frugality of ships, bicycles, and feet. Reclaiming
ownership of your time, not your vehicle.

At scale, the landscape reveals our values, becomes a map of our
hearts.

FIGURE 3. WHY IS THE SKY WHITE?

"We have so many allies in this world
that we aren't paying attention to
even just the color blue in the sky."
—David Whyte

Before solar radiation management
the sky was blue
as the first time
you opened your eyes.

The sky was blue because
it was mostly pairs of nitrogen atoms
absorbing a spectrum
but scattering blue
into your eyes.

In that sense the sky was
the color of union
of two invisibles dancing
at atmospheric scale
continuously above us
the sky was blue as love.

The sky was blue
as glacial lakes
when the mountains were
white with snow.

The sky was blue as truth
big enough to hold
both day and night at once

no one saw its fullness
but it was undeniable as breath
and just as fragile.

-

Now the sky is white
because we suspended particles there
like prayers like fog like disbelief
the world would hold us if we let go.

The sky is white
because we would not
fall from our daydream
because we could not imagine
a different thriving.

-

But our sunsets
are spectacular as the chemicals
bend sunlight into riots
that previously only appeared
when wildfires burned nearby.

Because beauty
can be pushed
to the edges of the Earth
but never defeated.

VIRUS

Who eats when we believe greed defines us?

The janitor installing nets below factory windows to catch jumpers—
or the marketing executive selling the phones assembled there?

A rising sea lifts all ships, its true,
but do you own a ship?
Do the climate refugees fleeing unlivable homes, seeking high ground
where wealth sequesters?

The night every human goes to bed with a full heart and belly,
capitalism starves by morning. It feeds on our discontents, needs us
distracted and numb. A successful virus does not kill its host too
quickly… as it deepens world hunger, widens inequality, liquidates
ecosystems for the lowest bidder, leaving us sick and overwhelmed.

Do you believe you are the virus? Or the host?

Who eats when we dream a higher hunger?
Everyone.

HUMAN

All stories you have been sold are false. As Buddhist teacher Pema Chodron reminds us, "there is no such thing as a true story" because all are made by humans weaving meaning from reality.

When we equate humanity with our colonizers—and not their indigenous resistors—we surrender a wealth of humanity to our smallest selves. When we place industrial culture at the zenith of human evolution, we ignore millennia spent exploring what it means to be human.

The market only recognizes us as alive while consuming. Reducing all that we are to this single identity makes us less alive, less human.

When we take what is not offered, we become thieves.
When we take without giving, we become parasites.
When we give ourselves freely to the Earth's pull,
when we yield to love,
we become fruit.

"You know whether a forest is healthy
by all the things it gives away."

–JANINE BENYUS
Biomimicry: Innovation Inspired by Nature

FRUIT

Actions ripen identity

Dependence

At its root, the word "dependence" means "to hang from". What could be more dependent than fruit—ripening by the grace of its stem?

Is it possible to imagine ourselves as fruit?

We certainly hang from the Earth: from a thread of breath to the water our cells swim in, the untold creatures inside our bodies and across our shared environments. Neighbor branches on a tree we would wither without.

Do we condemn ourselves as parasites because we must eat? There is no forgiving the knife we hold to our mother's throat, but if we opened to her unflinching love, grew larger than our greed, could we loosen our grip, drop our weapons and weep?

This rain waters a verdant return.

INTERDEPENDENCE

All concepts, even the existence of trees, are
pure imagination. I do not doubt the sensation
of my fingers on damp bark, but defining a
thing between leaves and root tips is a decision.
The seemingly obvious individuality of trees
is confused by unrelated neighbors grafting
themselves together,

the nitrogen-fixing lichens growing in their
branches that fall to the forest floor as fertilizer,
the intimacy of pollinators who shape entire life
cycles around species dependent on their services,
the microbiome trees rely upon to fight herbivory
and disease because they evolve over time scales
vastly greater than their threats,

the cellular apparatus of chloroplasts in each
leaf acquired from bacteria, the molecules trees
continuously exchange with the vapor bath of air
and moist circus of soil,
even the infinite non-being on either side of life.

Industrial culture encourages us to see ourselves as
individuals, separated by empty space, where other
cultures see an ocean of matter connecting all life.
Blaming ecocrisis on individual consumers distracts from
our power to unite and uproot industries responsible for
harm far beyond our own abilities.

GUILT

Guilt is seductive for the same reason it is ineffective: it narrows our gaze inward. The discord of our world is too complex for any one of us to fully grasp. The much simpler answer is to blame ourselves. Yet the further we isolate ourselves within our shame, the farther we are from the power of connection. We start to believe we are making the world a better place through self-flagellation. We become the very inertia we assume will defeat us.

Even after agreeing on the need to care for the world, we are often reluctant to include ourselves, our closest creature. It is still narcissism to believe we are unique in our worthlessness.

But tell me, do you think the world would be better off with more miserable people? Or more beings who have lit their lamp and share their light with the world?

GRACE

When I am tempted to wonder:
"am I worth the shadow I cast?
The fruit I pluck in hunger,
the ancient tissues I burn for movement,
to weave my synthetic sweater,
my casual disposal of eternal materials?

If I plant enough trees
could I erase myself?"

I visit the mango tree
and find no judgments,
just simple sensory evidence
of something other than fear:

"yes, even after all you have done
I offer my softest, sweetest flesh
without hesitation or condition."

Both dreams are true,
but which brings you alive?

GIFTS

On one level, the math is simple: we must sow more seeds than we reap or else we will exhaust the generosity of the Earth. It is a sign of our alienation from the living world how industrial culture struggles to imagine what this giving could look like.

And yet the answer is not hidden high in the towers of academia or deep in the caves of saints. Listen to the way bird song enriches the air. Watch how trees widen spirals of abundance: taking in air, water and nutrients, while also giving air, water and nutrients. Notice the feeling in your chest when you encounter an animal unexpectedly in the forest.

All of us are here
to give ourselves to one another.

Discovering our gifts is the work now ahead of us. We must look beyond industrial culture to explore what is possible, but we cannot simply appropriate indigenous cultures or become trees. Industrial culture requires its own reckoning.

FIGURE 4. ECO TERROR

"Eco" from the Greek "Oikos" meaning home

When the parking lot flooded
and the softball field
sucked our feet

as spring rains swelled
Dunawi creek
we celebrated small victories

of beavers reclaiming
paved wetlands
where they once swam.

At the dentist
numbness spread to my tongue
and lingered.

I don't know if
the pain we save
is always worth its cost:

opening my mouth to speak
breath receive a needle
a gamble between harm or healing.

The following night we found
the parking lot full of cars
and a cavity torn from the dam

by a city official,
the spectators speculated, through
binoculars searching blurs of urgent fur.

The sabotage shocked and reminded me
how most ecoterrorism operates
in uniform and broad daylight.

Why we harm ourselves
or any union of breathing earth
I may never understand,

but hear familiar slithers
of "necessity". When
the slender venom flute

slipped into my nerve
as a jagged flash
my eyes overflowed

suddenly confronted by all
I'd heaped inside.
The sound of running water

compels beavers to gnaw
down trees, drag them
in their jaws.

So we gathered
dusk after dusk
these newly mild evenings

to witness stick by stick
construction of a life's work,
clarity of purpose

we call "instinct" in other animals.
A week later, the city broke the dam again
and beavers resumed the same night.

I have touched the muck
where thoughts of giving up
one's red wet insides arise.

We are standing in it together
and I cannot dam
the rush of that pain.

I am telling you this
because beavers will need our help
rebuilding the Earth.

Because I know it is possible
to do what you must
while widening rivers of abundance.

My tongue was numb for months
but truthfully I have spent years
attempting to escape sensation

rather than return home
to a mind I have terrorized.
Slowly I'm relearning to taste

beauty as real as any fear. And
I believe in the budding revelry of green
as much as anything on Earth.

ENOUGH

There is no action anyone could take to heal all our shared wounds at once. It is easy to criticize a beach cleanup, recycling, or taking shorter showers as shallow expressions of environmental ethics, but these can be both necessary and insufficient.

The danger is not our smallness, but the pull of simple answers. If we use virtuous actions to justify future harm or inaction, our virtue may rebound. This is the difference between planting a tree to accrue moral credit to spend on future airline travel, or as one step along a lifelong commitment to ecological healing.

With intention, our small actions become a prayer, an invitation to deeper communion with life and our own abilities. This alternative to the insatiable search for "enough" leads along an endless path with more beauty and abundance than we can currently imagine.

Trees do not reach for light believing they will touch the source. They reach because doing so gives them life.

Cultivate

Often the puzzle of the world is put before us as if we should intuit the missing piece and make everything whole at once. A kinder and ultimately more realistic view is to consider the myriad benefits brought by a single action. Actions are grooved edges with places for further connection, rather than a border where change ends. Consider the act of planting a fruit tree...

Personal: Translating environmental anxiety into positive actions is a balm. Even simple contact with soil bacteria may improve mental health.

Temporal: Seedlings live where multiple scales of time meet and can be understood on a human scale. Planting affirms life now and invests in future opportunity.

Ecological: By providing resources for humans and other lives simultaneously, planting demonstrates small but real ways we can transcend zero-sum struggles.

Spiritual: Planting is neither purely metaphorical nor purely physical because it bears both fruits. Digging a hole to plant a tree creates an opening for life to enter us, for us to manifest the possibility of human benevolence.

KRUMMHOLZ

How tall could we have been in less severe soil?

I'm thinking not only of wind-twisted firs carving rootholds in alpine spines, but also humans bent against oppressive headwinds.

Scientists and poets dying of cholera, among the third of the world's people who still lack access to safe drinking water. All the women denied education, safety, political representation. Billions of us supporting hierarchy with our erosion.

Because we are the Earth, our imbalances are ecological as much as they are social. The willingness to exploit oil reserves or other humans share the same root. We cannot wait for one to stop before we address the other.

We have built entire economies on reckless extraction, unlivable wages, the dream of boundless growth. Our planet will not remain habitable unless we repay this debt, but leveling an unequal field is foremost the burden of those rooted in stolen loam.

Our mountains were built by accumulated choices, not tectonic uplift. When we choose simplicity for ourselves rather than force others towards scarcity, we better hear the purity of birdsong in thin air.

UNDERSTORY

Asking all nations to reduce emissions is often criticized as unfair. Wealthy nations of the world burned fossilized sunlight with abandon, and now we have the audacity to ask Nigeria and India to reduce their emissions?

But is it truly equitable to encourage poor countries to follow the wealthy through their dirty slog of development? Should we encourage Indonesia to protect its forests by deforesting Japan? Should West Africans capture North American farmers for their sorghum fields?

The first trees in an open space easily exploit the abundant sunlight. The trees that follow would wither in shadow if they were not nursed through a community of roots.

What if justice looked like mutual aid, rather than an encore of moral failure? What if poor countries began a massive investment in regenerative infrastructure, paid for by the countries with the longest record of profiting from planetary degradation. Not a token amount constituting a "sorry-you're-late-to-the-party" favor, but such a large portion of GDP that wealthy nations can no longer afford extravagant military or fossil fuel subsidies.

Equity is not pity. A forest is stronger and more beautiful when each tree is given what it needs to reach its fullest expression.

FIGURE 5. ENDEMIC

or

An open letter from the Devil's Hole Pupfish
regarding funding for an ongoing effort
to save the species from extinction

We are thirty-five fish in a single pool
you call "Devil's Hole", National Park, Nevada.
This the only home we've ever known.

Human efforts brought us back from the brink
of extinction, but some of you still wonder,
"why bother with such a little fish?"

-

We were not given the cleverness to invent
the atomic weapons you tested in our desert
or the wells drinking the aquifer beneath our pool

and yet we found this crevasse without assistance
of legs or wings, measuring 72 feet long by 11 feet wide
and deeper than any human knows:

the smallest range of any spined creature.
How much is an unsolved mystery worth to you?
How much is one answer worth

to the question "why are we here?"
How much would you pay
for proof that life is possible

in Earth's most marginal places?
Can't you see Earth
is also one blue pool?

Do you truly believe you have found a place
on life's tapestry
where the fraying edge will never reach you?

We are not your children, you must remember.
We did not ask for your guardianship, we fell
into your hands because you took our lifeblood

for yours. Is our upkeep a greater burden
than adding another ghost to your menagerie?
After how many erasures is restitution due?

This is our only request:
do not collect us as curios of a dying planet.
Return the treasures you have taken.

DOING

Most ecological damage is caused by what humans *are doing* not by what we have *failed to do*. Salmon migrations are thwarted by dams, not a lack of fish ladders.

Recovering wildlife populations across the world demonstrate that for some species, from whales to beavers and wolves, healing begins as soon as we set down our weapons.

Whether we choose to solve more problems or cause fewer will determine our reach for low hanging fruits like emissions reductions or unripe technologies like solar radiation management. Our most powerful responses are frequently dismissed as untenable because they require a willingness to change ourselves, rather than continue changing the planet.

Filling fewer wetlands to expand suburbs or clearing less rainforest for cattle pasture cannot be our endgame, however. Aiming for zero will at best slow the death of our planet. Decreasing the frantic quantity of our efforts leaves more oxygen for their quality.

Taking a breath, we can move beyond reducing our footprints treading on the Earth, and start to increase our handprints, lifting life up.

BEING

The quality of your presence determines the seeds you sow.

Cultivating the being that radiates beneath all our identities and actions is not a luxury reserved for wealthy white environmentalists, it is a power given to every human, every tree, every being.

A grove that is burned, infested, or cut will not have access to the same reach of seeds as one flourishing in diversity, will not be able to participate fully in surrounding restoration efforts.

Healing your inner landscape is not a distraction from global ecocrisis, it is the most intimate access you have to our shared poison.

Becoming the peace you seek is not a retreat from trouble, it is the hardest work you will ever do.

INTELLIGENCE

The complex network of mycelia underneath a forest has been compared to the human brain, both because of its structure and the way it sends chemical messages between nodes. Neurons and trees even share a similar form. Some cry anthropomorphism at this comparison, yet they could hardly be farther from truth.

Trees do not embody human intelligence. Rater, intelligence manifests in resonant patterns throughout diverse life forms. The intelligence of forest networks is not approaching a human mind, it is a separate reach into the depths of consciousness. Just as dolphins, elephants, crows, and slime molds have all evolved unique means of perceiving and responding to the world around them. Because there is no one answer, intelligence is not a ladder to the sun, but rays radiating outward.

When we equate all intelligence with humanity, we ignore the wealth of information accumulated before us: how to divide cells, how to build proteins, how to sense light, sound, molecules, how to recognize danger, how to hold one another. Our innovations are meaningful, like a frontal cortex and bipedal mobility, but a flower should not become so enamored with its petals that it forgets the tree from which it blooms.

MICROCLIMATE

Does consciousness rest in individual trees, or does it emerge from the connections between them, at the forest scale? Is one neuron conscious, or only the web it exists in?

Despair is easy, watching the torment we continue to share with one another. It can be hard to fathom one burning river, one mass shooting... except to say the world is cruel.

What do you find when you examine your own mind, fumbling deep into the dark soil? In stillness, what visits you? A pure self-knowing, or a cacophony of thoughts, sensations, voices that don't belong to you?

Climb into the canopy and look on the forest of humanity. Can you differentiate between your own or another's storm-shaken struggle for light?

Whether you are a branch, a tree, a forest, a vein of lightning, the work remains the same.

BRANCHES

We have allowed ourselves to believe we can reach heaven climbing the backs we have broken, as if leaves could reach the sky without the branches carrying them.

In the canopy, we see for ourselves there is only sky above us. Heaven becomes a horizon we move towards, a place we cannot arrive without bringing the whole world with us.

What at eye-level appears as one steady trunk, becomes unity reaching out in all directions. Overcoming anthropocentrism, racism, patriarchy, any division, it becomes clear what we are reaching for is the flourishing of life in all its forms. Our harm can then be measured by the space we take from others to become their fullest selves.

CROWN

Conflict recedes when given a high enough view. In this one universe, this continuous moment, there is nothing we can steal from one another or from the future that could be regained in a separate universe or distant moment.

The ends have always lived in our minds, only the means have ever been in our hands.

Climbing higher still, above even the desire to change the world, we are called purely to witness to the mystery we swim within.

This is a place to return whenever ecocrisis begins to feel like a political position or nostalgia for an unreclaimable past. Our umbilical connection to beauty, to awe, to the whole living world is not an abstract or contentious ideal.

It is essential to our being.

"Even if I knew that tomorrow the world would go to pieces,
I would still plant my apple tree."
—MARTIN LUTHER

HUMUS

Our World's End

COMPOST

The absence of waste in forest systems suggests there may yet be some use for the mess we've made. In the mid 1990's truckloads of orange peels from a Costa Rican juice factory were dumped on a degraded field. At first, environmentalists decried the industrial negligence, but after a few years scientists returned to the field and measured a lush forest, showing greater growth and diversity than adjacent plots left undisturbed.

Rather than burn everything to the ground,
it may be possible to break down what no longer serves us
as soil does: disassemble dying systems,
repurpose its elements into new life
through the tireless work
of innumerable creatures
with small, brief lives.

NURSE LOG

It is not alarmist to admit the human species will end one day. All things end. Instead, we should consider what "survival" looks like within the broader reality of impermanence.

We have for too long, told life's story as a straight path from the big bang to humanity. Within this arc, the whole universe flickers out once the last human dies.

Yet we can see this is not the case with other organisms. Trees for example, often support more life as they decay than they did while growing. A living tree might be less than ten percent living tissue, supported by a lifeless structure of wood. When it falls to the forest floor it hosts a banquet of new beginnings.

We cannot fully imagine the intricate ways consciousness will flower if given space, but we do know that something will follow us. Will we spend our time on Earth enriching the soil that nurtured us even if what grows is more than human?

Rootstock

While grafting, I sever the central stem of my trees. Yet when grafts fail to take, the trees consistently respond by initiating new shoots.

I've seen this same behavior in trees struck by lightning or toppled in a landslide. Maybe inwardly they protest the labor of healing or the unfairness of their circumstances. Outwardly, at least, the will to live persists until the last molecule of sugar is spent.

This rootedness may arise from an inability to flee, but produces a commitment to sit with the pain, to stay with the world we have, that legged creatures struggle to mirror.

Demanding we address the root causes of ecocrisis is among the hardest requests we can make. A seedling's courage offers an alternative to despair: no matter how wicked our problems, hope can be just as tenacious.

Scion

Planting seeds from a Hass avocado, Alphonso mango, or Pink Pearl apple will not produce a tree with the same fruit. Offspring are often stringy, bitter, or occasionally sensational. We choose our intentions, but not their yield.

Humans have learned to cut buds from remarkable individuals and graft them with compatible stems. In this way, we have spread fruit with the most desirable flavor, color, size, hardiness, and many other dimensions.

This union allows for roots adapted to local conditions, supporting branches of reliable abundance. It is possible to participate in global community and share our sweetest discoveries, without surrendering what makes place irreplaceable.

Because hunger has endless answers.

Neglect

When agricultural scientist Masanobu Fukuoka inherited his family's orchard, he was so enamored with the elegance of nature he decided to let the trees take care of themselves. The orchard quickly became tangled and riddled with pests, forcing Fukuoka to admit his neglect. Eventually he developed a system of natural farming that draws on the strengths of each species to create resilient ecosystems, just as productive as his neighbor's fields dependent on chemicals and heavy machinery.

Like Fukuoka, we are also looking upon an orchard, shaped by human hands and minds. At least 97% of Earth's surface has now been impacted by human activity. This leads to two truths:
we cannot walk away and
we cannot stay here alone.

Because humans did not invent suffering, we cannot take it with us in our spaceship and leave the Earth in peace. We cannot extinguish the wildfire by fleeing.

Instead of escape, we can stay and nurture more-than-human flourishing. We can call on the strengths of every creature: our own gifts of imagination, alongside the alchemy of fungus, the sequestration forests, the protective powers of wetlands, the generosity of sunlight. Every one of us.

ACCEPT

A mind that can imagine more beautiful futures can tear itself to pieces digging through the bones of our world. We must not let the ferocity of our dreams be misconstrued as weakness, as illness.

A human that can tear the world to pieces cannot be called powerless. It is too late to pretend surrender, standing in a clearcut while claiming we cannot make a difference.

With our power beyond question, we are invited
into the endless forest of cultural evolution,
armed with only the courage we carry and
what love we summon from our given breaths.

Throw down the burden and it will not break,
        take it up and know the simplest thing:

you exist.

RESIST

Resistance shapes a river
even more than the water itself.
Boulders and fallen logs
determine the pools

and meander, riffles stir
sparkling oxygen,
and runs unbuild mountains
one stone at a time.

Slowness allows fish to spawn,
dragged ashore by bears
their bones fertilize the trees
that fall and enrich the banks further.

We throw our lives into the river
not in defiance of progress
but to demand a flood:
swell beyond lines dividing

who grows and who erodes.
Everything you know and love
the sea will reclaim, will flow downstream.
Yet life remains, and widens

through the friction our dreams provide.
Our struggle is not against
our small deaths,
but to claim larger lives.

SUSTAIN

If a friend told you their relationship to their partner was "sustainable," you'd probably have some follow up questions. But what about joy? Discovery? Do they bring you alive?

If your friend told you their relationship to the planet was "sustainable," you should be concerned for the same reasons.

Finding a way to remain in an abusive relationship with the planet for as long as possible is not an acceptable definition of success.

Either we collectively imagine and enact a more loving way of being... or we cease to be.

FIGURE 6. PLENUM

To be heard while humming

My first breath of air
was a cry of terror
I was so bewildered
by every miracle

entering my senses
and have since been
pretending otherwise
but why?

I learned to ignore
the refrigerator's hum,
gathered continuums
into discrete red yellow blues,

I counted all the ways
we are different
and was swallowed
by infinity. I counted

all the ways we are different
and came up empty.
At first sight
our love was so simple:

cosmos, particular
woman, flower.
I measured your petals
with metal instruments

when I could have been
busy making music with bees.
We supplied answers
exactly as wet and granular

as sandcastles
and twice as fragile.
We asked questions
exactly as wet and necessary

as sandwiches
and twice as toothsome.
We kicked and screamed
against our few Earthly certainties

like inevitable death
and our irrefutable beauty.
I believe you feel
the Earth is hurting,

but they need
your grief as much
as your songs, your prayers
as much as your silence.

Before you despair
feel the air
separating us, believe
we are broken.

Feel the air
weaving our breath together,
believe
we are whole.

ENDURE

Living trees have watched most of the world's wetlands drained, grasslands converted to crops, forests devoured, entire mountains toppled, plastics choking the ocean, once bountiful animals dwindling to fragmented habitats.

Many of them have lived long enough to witness orchestrated madness spill across the world in a war to end all wars. And then, only a few decades later, a second World War. Rivalries emerging from those ashes invented weapons capable of destroying all life on Earth.

The oldest living trees, the bristlecones, cypress, and yews approaching 5,000 years have seen many empires rise and fall. Some clonal aspen and oaks are much older than the birth of agriculture, everything under the freighted word "civilization".

Imagine how many storms they've weathered over millennia, branches snapping and trunk groaning, uncertain of the dawn. How many leaves they have offered, knowing the wind will take them?

In every twist and scar would you read brokenness and defeat? Or a testament to all that can be survived?

.

FLOURISH

Our world is a thicket of paradox. Without a clear path forward, it is easy to lose our way and wander to the twin clearings of denial or cynicism. There is a sense of relief in knowing that either nothing needs fixing or everything is so broken there is no sense trying to fix it.
But both are such small windows to an infinite sky.

One alternative is to choose paths that remain true, no matter where they lead you.

Do we need every detail of apocalypse to know if our next step should be made in kindness or hatred? If we lose the coral in 20 years or 50 years, isn't our work the same? Will you ever look back on the extinction of bees and think, "at least we didn't strive too hard"?

Apocalypse isn't what scares us the most. Even more terrifying is the possibly of flourishing. Because, if we allowed ourselves to believe we could succeed, could become more fully alive, our collective soul would not let us rest until we threw our every breath, our identities, all that we own, against the comfort of our doubt.

THE END

It is easy to see the world is ending. You can watch multi-million-dollar films portray every lurid detail. You can read the news or a book about the environment. But before you hunker into your underground bunker, consider informing your neighbors.

Tell the barley farmers of Tibet how concerned you are that fresh water is becoming scarce as they watch the glacier above their village melt faster year after year.

Warn an American Elm tree about rapid deforestation—two thirds of tropical rainforests already gone—as they watch their siblings fall: Chestnuts, Ash, Redwoods and the rest.

Tell the Kenyan cattle herder of the looming dangers of unstable weather as he boards a bus to Nairobi to look for work because he lost too many cows in last year's drought.

When someone warns you the world is ending, ask them, "who's world?" Listen for the tremble in the voices of those who have accumulated the most to lose by swallowing other worlds as their belly gurgles and churns with worry.

Figure 7. Dawn is a Place in the Sky

above all of this
dawn is one ongoing phenomenon

I saw it
from airplane windows

as salmon honey spilled
over a cloud meadow

looking down at Earth
where night and day

are considered
separate ephemera

I saw clearly we
have always been on

the precipice of darkness
always at morning's door

I do not say the world
is ending or a new world

is being born out
of despair or hope

just the truth
of immutable revolutions

LIMINAL

We have always imagined ourselves at history's edge,
peering over the precipice
                    at our unwritten future.

What would falling look like
if not ice melting
to expose new arctic oil reserves?
If not seas swallowing the lowest island,
then another and another?
If not a city in its richest moment
full of people with no place to sleep?

Letting go of the ledge, could we embrace this generative space?
Abundance flows where elements meet: from the unrivaled diversity of
coral reefs in shallow coastal waters to the tallest trees along California's
fog belt, the birdsong at the edge of dawn to the skin of soil stitched
between air and bedrock. The literal ends of our Earth.

There is no distance between history and dreams,
between crisis and opportunity,
between apocalypse and utopia.

Fruit is both death and rebirth.

The Beginning

Humans have predicted imminent endings for thousands of years because ends have always existed within human potential. When we accept this will always be true, we are invited to lift our gaze from the smallness of short-term survival. With our heads down, we are unable to see more beautiful futures far ahead of us.

So much has been lost,
but look around and see everyone else is also here and we have something to give one another. Each of us has unlimited kindness, attention, curiosity, generosity, as well as hatred, greed, violence, and everything else. Everything you believe in exists in this single shared moment.

We cannot stop the sunset any more than we can stop the sunrise. We can instead, turn to the precious soil of this moment. The difficult soil, the only soil.

We are fruit. We contain the seeds of all possible futures. Then we realize the beginning of the world is also happening now.

Planting seeds will never be an end,
but it will always be a place to begin.

The future is bleak
as our apathy

and boundless
as our love.

Sources

Introduction

Livingston, Frederick. "Planting Trees as a Bridge Between Material and Spiritual Responses to Environmental Crisis." *Journal of Agriculture and Human Values* (2021).

Dreams

Harari, Yuval Noah. *Sapiens: A Brief History of Humankind.* Harper, 2015.

Coates, Ta-Nehisi. *Between the World and Me.* Random House, 2017: "…racism is a visceral experience, [it] dislodges brains, blocks airways, rips muscle, extracts organs, cracks bones, breaks teeth. You must never look away from this."

Wengrow, David and Graeber, David. *The Dawn of Everything: A New History of Humanity.* Farrar, Straus and Giroux, 2021.

Chazdon et al. "When is a forest a forest? Forest concepts and definitions in the era of forest and landscape restoration." *Ambio* 45.5 (2016): 538–550.

Services

Barnaud, C., & Antona, M. "Deconstructing ecosystem services: Uncertainties and controversies around a socially constructed concept." *Geoforum* 56 (2014): 113–123.

Clark, B. & York, R. "Carbon Metabolism: Global capitalism, climate change, and the biospheric rift." *Theory and Society* (2005).

Ellison, D., Martyn N. Futter and K. Bishop. "On the forest cover–water yield debate: from demand- to supply-side thinking." *Global Change Biology* 18.3 (2011): 806-820.

Garvin E.C., Cannuscio C.C., Branas C.C. "Greening vacant lots to reduce violent crime: a randomized controlled trial." *Injury Prevention* 19 (2013): 198-203.

Kuo, F. E., & Sullivan, W. C. "Aggression and Violence in the Inner City: Effects of Environment via Mental Fatigue." *Environment and Behavior* 33.4 (2001): 543-571.

Haluza, D., Schönbauer, R., & Cervinka, R. 2014. "Green Perspectives for Public Health: A Narrative Review on the Physiological Effects of Experiencing Outdoor Nature." *International Journal of Environmental Research and Public Health* 11.5 (2014).

Tsunetsugu, Y., Park, B.J., & Miyazaki, Y. "Trends in Research Related to "Shinrin-yoku" (taking in the forest atmosphere or forest bathing) in Japan." *Environ Health Prev Med* 15.27 (2009).

Kaplan, S. *The Restorative Environment: Nature and Human Experiences.* University of Michigan, 1992.

Sacred

Narayanan, V. "Water, Wood, and Wisdom: Ecological Perspectives from the Hindu Traditions." *Daedalus: Journal of the American Academy of Arts and Sciences* 130 (2001): 179-206.

Dwivedi, O. P. and Tiwari, B.N. "Environmental Protection in the Hindu Religion." *Ethical Perspectives on Environmental Issues in India.* A.P.H Publishing Corporation, 1999.

Swearer, D. K. "Principles and Poetry, Places and Stories: The Resources of Buddhist Ecology." *Daedalus: Journal of the American Academy of Arts and Sciences* 130 (2001): 225-241.

Bayrak, M.M. & Marafa, L.M. "Ten years of REDD+: A critical review of the impact of REDD+ on forest-dependent communities." *Sustainability* (2016).

War

Perfecto, I., Vandermeer, J. H., & Wright, A.L. "Nature's matrix: linking agriculture, conservation and food sovereignty." *Earthscan* (2009).

Russel, Edmund. *War and Nature: fighting humans and insects with chemicals from world war I to silent spring.* Cambridge University Press, 2001.

FAO, "Scaling up agroecology initiative," United Nations, 2018.

Bocarejo, D. & Ojeda, D. "Violence and conservation: Beyond unintended consequences and unfortunate coincidences." *Geoforum* 69 (2016): 176-183.

Duffy, R. "Waging a war to Save Biodiversity: the rise of militarized conservation." *International Affairs* 90.4 (2014): 819-834.

Change

Erlanger, Steven. "After 2,000 Years, a Seed from Ancient Judea Sprouts." *New York Times*, 2005.

Kimmerer, Robin Wall. Gathering Moss: A Natural and Cultural History of Mosses. OSU Press, 2003.

Solnit, Rebecca. Hope in the Dark: Untold Histories, Wild Possibilities. Haymarket Books, 2016.

Trees

Ball, J. "Why Carbon Pricing Isn't Working." *Foreign Affairs* (2018): 134-146.

Marin, R. A., & Janiola, M. D. C. "Carbon Sequestration Potential of Fruit Tree Plantations in Southern Philippines." *Journal of Biodiversity and Environmental Sciences* (JBES) 8.5 (2016): 164–174.

Meyfroidt, P., and E.F. Lambin. "Global Forest Transition: Prospects for an End to Deforestation." *Annual Review of Environment and Resources* 36 (2011): 343–371.

Matthew Sturm, M. Douglas, T. Racine, C. Liston, G. "Changing snow and shrub conditions affect albedo with global implications." *Journal of Geophysical Research* (2005).

Tragedy

Hardin, G. "The Tragedy of the Commons." *Science* 162.3859 (1968): 1243-1248.

Diamond, Jared. *Collapse: how societies choose to fail or succeed*. Viking Press, 2005.

McAnany, Norman Yofee & Patricia Ann. *Questioning Collapse: Human Resilience, Ecological Vulnerability, and the Aftermath of Empire*. Cambridge University Press, 2009.

Galeano, Eduardo. *Open Veins of Latin America: Five Centuries of the Pillage of a Continent*. Monthly Review Press, 1997.

Breed

Ehrlich PR, Ehrlich AH. "Can a collapse of global civilization be avoided?" *Royal Society* 280.1754 (2013).

Planet of the Humans. Dir. J. Gibbs. Rumble Media. 2020.

World Bank, "2019 CO2 Emissions (metric tons per capita)," data. worldbank.org.

> Note: I used 14.7 tons CO2/yr per American and 0.2 tons CO2/yr per Afghani. China's total emissions at 10.7 billion tons CO2/yr and Africa at 648 million tons CO2/yr.

Starr, D. "Just 90 Companies are to blame for most of climate change, this 'carbon accountant' says". *Science.org*, 2016.

Feed

Jeavons, John. *How to Grow More Vegetables: Than You Ever Thought Possible on Less Land with Less Water Than You Can Imagine.* Ten Speed Press, 2017.

> Note: these calculations come from 5.34 million square miles of arable land. With highly developed skill and soil, a complete diet can be produced in as little as 1,000 square feet. With this rate, the planet could theoretically support over 148 billion humans.

United Nations. "Our Growing Population." 2023.

Livingston, Frederick. "Waging Peace on Hunger." *Ideas for Peace* (2021).

Conserve

Temudo, M. "The White Men Bought the Forests: Conservation and Contestation in Guinea-Bissau." *Conservation and Society* (2012).

Ostrom, Elinor. *Governing the Commons.* Cambridge University Press, 1990.

Paquette, A., & Messier, C. "The role of plantations in managing the world's forests in the Anthropocene." *Frontiers in Ecology and the Environment* (2010).

Fifanou, V. G., Ousmane, C., Gauthier, B., & Brice, S. "Traditional agroforestry systems and biodiversity conservation in Benin (West Africa)." *Agroforestry Systems* 82 (2011): 1-13.

Kimmerer, Robin Wall. Braiding *Sweetgrass: indigenous wisdom, scientific knowledge, and the teachings of plants.* Milkweed Press, 2013.

Good

Mann, Charles C. *1491: New Revelations of the Americas Before Columbus*. Vintage, 2006.

Jeavons, John. "Biointensive Sustainable Mini-Farming: II. Perspective, Principles, Techniques and History." *Sustainable Agriculture* 19.2 (2001): 65-76.

Penniman, Leah. *Farming While Black: Soul Fire Farm's Practical Guide to Liberation on the Land*. Chelsea Green, 2018.

Lancaster, Brad. *Rainwater Harvesting for Drylands*. Rainsource Press, 2013.

Dragon-Smith, C., T. P. DeCouto, & A. Carvill. "Balancing worldviews: Climate Change Solutions in Canada's North." 2020.

Symbiosis

Sheldrake, Merlin. *Entangled Life: How Fungi Make Our Worlds, Change Our Minds & Shape Our Futures*. Random House, 2020.

Georgia C. Drew, Emily J. Stevens & Kayla C. King. "Microbial evolution and transitions along the parasite–mutualist continuum." *Nature Reviews Microbiology* 19 (2021).

Innovation

Jackson, Tim. "Prosperity without growth: economics for a finite planet." *Earthscan*, 2009.

Values

FAO. "FAO warns 90 per cent of Earth's topsoil at risk by 2050." 2022.

Braungart, Michael & McDonough, William. *The Upcycle: Beyond Sustainability: Designing for Abundance*. North Point Press, 2013.

FAO, IFAD, UNICEF, WFP and WHO. *The State of Food Security and Nutrition in the World*. Rome: FAO, 2019.

Zucman, Gabriel. "Global Wealth Inequality." *Annual Review of Economics* 11 (2019): 109-138.

Virus

Ye, Juliet. "Foxconn Installs Antijumping Nets at Hebei Plants." *Wallstreet Journal* (2010).

Lipsky, Laura van Dernoot. The *Age of Overwhelm: Strategies for the Long Haul.* Berrett-Koehler, 2018.

Interdependence

Pillai, Swaminathan Chitraputhira and Palani, Nivethadevi. "Inosculation in Trees - A Spiritual Perspective." *SSRN* (2021).

Corinne, V., Bastien, C., Emmanuelle, J. et al. "Trees and Insects Have Microbiomes: Consequences for Forest Health and Management." *Current Forestry Report* 7 (2021): 81–96.

Abram, David. *Spell of the Sensuous: Perception and Language in a More than Human World.* Vintage Books, 2017.

Guilt

Taranath, Anu. *Beyond Guilt Trips: mindful travel in an unequal world.* AK Press, 2019.

Enough

Wapner, P. & Willoughby, J. "The irony of environmentalism: the ecological futility but political necessity of lifestyle change." *Ethics & International Affairs* 19.3 (2005): 77-89.

Dütschke E., Frondel M., Schleich J. and Vance C. "Moral Licensing—Another Source of Rebound?" *Front. Energy Res.* 6.38 (2018)

Cultivate

C.A. Lowry et al. "Identification of an immune-responsive mesolimbocortical serotonergic system: potential role in regulation of emotional behavior." *Neuroscience* (2007).

Krummholz

World Health Organization. "1 in 3 people globally do not have access to safe drinking water" – UNICEF, WHO. Geneva: News Release, 2019.

Doing

Preston, Christopher. *Tenacious Beasts: Wildlife Recoveries That Change How We Think about Animals.* MIT Press, 2023.

Intelligence

Money, N.P. "Hyphal and mycelial consciousness: the concept of the fungal mind." Fungal Biology 125 (2021): 257-259.

Simard, Suzanne. *Finding the Mother Tree.* Knopf, 2021.

Compost

Treuer, T. L. H., Choi, J. J., Janzen, D. H., Hallwachs, W., Peréz-Aviles, D., Dobson, A. P., Wilcove, D. S. "Low-cost agricultural waste accelerates tropical forest regeneration." *Restoration Ecology* 26.2 (2017): 275–283.

Neglect

Fukuoka, M. *One Straw Revolution: an Introduction to Natural Farming.* Rodale Press, 1978.

Andrew J. Plumptre et al. "Where Might We Find Ecologically Intact Communities?" *Frontiers in Forests and Global Change* (2021).

Flourish

CrimethInc Workers Collective. *Days of Love Nights of War: Crimethink for Beginners.* 2001.

The End

Krogh, Anders. "State of the Tropical Rainforest." www.regnskog.no/en/news. 2020.

Acknowledgments

These pages passed through my hands
between all the gifts I have been given
and you: the soil that will receive them.

Specifically, I am grateful to the Huetar people,
who carried the land
where the University for Peace now stands.

I am grateful for all the teachers:
friends who saved their avocado pits
and sweated over shovels with me,
trees who made me sick with fruit,
the professors who watered our questions.

I am alive because of the air
water, sunlight alchemy, love
from others. But also you, the soil,
where my seeds might sprout
and prove the truth of abundance.

"Endemic" and "Dawn is a Place in the Sky" previously appeared in
Pamplemousse, Volume 4 Issue 2, May 2023

"Eco Terror" previously appeared in *Antler Velvet Arts Journal*, January
2024.

About the Author

Frederick Livingston grew from the southern tip of the Salish Sea in Olympia, Washington. He has since studied and practiced sustainable agriculture, experiential education, and peace building across the world. He is the author of the poetry collection *The Moon and Other Fruits* (Legacy Book Press, 2023) as well as numerous poems and articles. He holds a master's degree in environment, development, and peace from the United Nations Mandated University for Peace in Costa Rica.

WWW.FREDERICKLIVINGSTON.COM

homebound
PUBLICATIONS

Homebound Publications is a Trans/Queer Owned publishing house based in the Berkshire Mountains. What began during a brainstorming session in a Boston cafe has become a platform for hundreds of indie authors. More than a company, we are a community of writers and readers exploring the larger questions we face as a global village. We publish full-length works of creative non-fiction and poetry.

homeboundpublications.com

WAYFARER

BASED IN THE BERKSHIRE MOUNTAINS, MASS.

At Wayfarer Books we believe poetry is the language of the earth. We believe words—shaped like rivers through wild places—can change the shape of the world. We publish poets and writers and renegades who stand outside of mainstream culture—poets, essayists, and storytellers whose work might withstand the scrutiny of crows and coyotes, those who are cryptic and floral, the crepuscular, and the queer-at-heart. We are more than just a publisher but a community of writers. Our mission is to produce books that can serve as a compass and map to all wayfarers through wild terrain.

WAYFARERBOOKS.ORG

www.ingramcontent.com/pod-product-compliance
Lightning Source LLC
Chambersburg PA
CBHW031433120626
46545CB00006B/2385